SPIRITUAL HEALING

SPIRITUAL HEALING

SWAMI PARAMANANDA

GYAN

Published by

GYAN

Gyan Publishing House
5, Ansari Road
Daryaganj, New Delhi-110002
Phone: 011-47034999, 9811692060
E-mail: books@gyanbooks.com

Distribution Network
gyanbooks.com
India, USA, Canada, UK, Australia

ISBN: 978-93-6433-034-3 (HB)
First Published, 1923

2nd Impression 2024

Printed at: Gyan Press, Delhi.

SPIRITUAL HEALING
Author: SWAMI PARAMANANDA

Practical Series No. 4

Spiritual Healing

Spiritual Healing

BY
SWAMI PARAMANANDA

AUTHOR OF "SOUL'S SECRET DOOR," "REINCARNATION AND IMMORTALITY," "SELF-MASTERY," "VEDANTA IN PRACTICE," "CONCENTRATION AND MEDITATION," ETC.

REVISED AND ENLARGED EDITION

PUBLISHED BY
THE VEDANTA CENTRE
BOSTON, MASS., U. S. A.

CONTENTS

Soul's Physician

MY life's wounds are healed at Thy touch,
O Thou, my soul's Physician!
Never had I hoped for such benediction,
But Thou, divine Healer, knowing my heart's prayer didst come of Thine own compassion.
My spirit was broken,—it is mended now;
I am made whole at Thy approach;
I have no life apart from Thee;
I am bound to Thee now and forevermore!

(This poem is reprinted from "Soul's Secret Door," by the same author.)

I.

SPIRITUAL HEALING

Know That to be indestructible by which all this is pervaded. No one is ever able to destroy that Immutable.—*Bhagavad-Gita.*

Court not death in the error of your life; neither draw upon yourselves destruction by the works of your hands; because God made not death; neither delighteth He when the living perish; for righteousness is immortal.—*Wisdom of Solomon.*

IS cure of disease possible and practical by other than medical means? If there is a particle of Truth in mental or spiritual healing, we must not only cease to be antagonistic towards it, but must welcome it with our whole heart. This world is full of suffering and if any one can bring relief, we should not care through what channel it comes. In order to investigate these vital problems of life we must be willing to put aside our preconceived ideas and prejudices, and take an attitude of openness and fairness. In all the Sacred Writings of the world accounts are given of supernatural cures. Healing of the sick, raising of the dead, driving out of evil spirits; these are not peculiar to the life of Jesus the Christ, but are to be found in the lives of all the great Saviours, Prophets, Saints and Seers. There is one type of mind which regards all these narratives as absurd and imaginary, designed to misguide the ignorant; there is another type which is over-credulous and inclined to magnify all such accounts, regarding them as special miracles, possible only to certain divinely appointed ones. But intellectual scepticism cannot help us, neither can blind acceptance. Our attitude should be neither to discredit nor to support on hearsay, but to investigate and learn the truth.

In the Vedic Scriptures we are told that the soul of man is beyond all mortal afflictions; that it "is free from sin, free from old age, free from death and grief, free from hunger and thirst." These words open another vista. Are we then not what we believe ourselves to be? Are these bodily conditions unreal? No; our physical life is not unreal, but it does not constitute the whole of our being. In fact, it represents but a very small part of our real life. Unfortunately to the majority of us it seems the largest part; and it is through such misconceptions that we block the steady flow of our life-force and suffer in endless ways. Disease always indicates disturbance and disorder; and disorder invariably results when our physical tendencies lead us away from the direct influence of the soul, or when our bodily desires gain ascendancy over our spiritual nature. If it is true, however, that the vital part of our life is unchangeable, unaffected by suffering and disease, what is it we see around us? We recognize disease, we recognize suffering; for nearly all of us these pains and ailments are facts, while that unchangeable Reality seems at most a dream.

There is no doubt that physical science has done a great deal to help mankind. It has brought relief; but that relief is not permanent, because the elements with which it deals are not permanent. It does not reach the cause of the misery; nor does it apply the ultimate remedy. Through the power of Spirit man lives! The real seat of disease is more often in the mind than in the body. We know how our mental attitude can have a devitalizing influence on our physical constitution and also how it can energize it. When we are not well, we often try a change of climate; the same kind of inward change is even more helpful—change of thought. If we can leave behind all thought of disease, that is the best way of eliminating it. By this method we forget the body and thereby lift ourselves out of the condition. But we cannot do this so long as we believe that our existence is dependent on this body. We must realize that we are born of Spirit and sustained by Spirit, and therefore nothing can prevail against us. It is because we have lost this higher point of view and drifted away that we feel helpless and ailing.

The only true healing is accomplished by contact with the spiritual essence; but this cannot be done in a professional way. I believe in spiritual healing. I have seen too many instances of it to doubt it. One may not believe in prayer, but prayer heals. Faith also has great healing power, because it elevates us to a plane where we can be healed. There are many, many instances of this in India. Men who have been pronounced incurable by physicians have made a long journey to touch the feet of a holy man or bathe in a sacred river or pray at a certain shrine, believing firmly that they will thereby be cured, and they have been. Whence comes this power? All power is of the Spirit. Through whole-hearted prayer and unwavering faith we succeed in making ourselves receptive to this power. Unless we are open to its direct influence, it cannot penetrate our being and heal us.

We see in Christ's life that He was not able to help all the people who came in contact with Him, but only those who had unquestioning faith. In St. Matthew we read: "And when Jesus departed thence, two blind men followed Him, crying and saying, Thou Son of David, have mercy on us. And when He was come into the house the blind men came to Him, and Jesus saith unto them: Believe ye that I am able to do this? They said unto Him, yea, Lord. Then touched He their eyes saying, According to your faith be it unto you. And their eyes were opened." Again He spoke thus to the woman who had touched the hem of His garment: Daughter, be of good comfort; thy faith hath made thee whole. And the woman was made whole from that hour. Also to the Centurion He said: As thou hast believed, so be it unto thee. This absolute faith is the basis of all healing; even in medical science it is necessary; but it is not that kind of faith which is identified with indiscrimination and ignorance. We must always differentiate between faith and blind belief. Faith springs from purity of heart, from direct perception. As the soul recognizes the power of God over all things and seeks to be restored by that power, a connection is established and healing is accomplished.

The Scriptures tell us that disease is the result of sin. Some define sin as wrong thinking, others as wrong doing; but whatever definition we accept, it is apparent that when we go against nature, we create certain results from which we cannot escape. But why do good people and innocent children suffer? Those who ask this question do not take into account that no life begins here and now. What comes here may be the result of mistakes in previous lives. Also suffering is often a great purifying agent. Through how many hardships and painful experiences have great Souls had to pass in order to attain their greatness! Even sickness sometimes proves a blessing. It all depends on the mental attitude with which we meet it. If we allow ourselves to be dragged down and made despondent and unhappy by it, then it becomes a misfortune; otherwise it may be the means of bringing to us a new spiritual awakening.

We must analyze and find out what is

our real nature. We must ask ourselves: "What part of myself is my true Self? Is it my hands or my feet? Is it my mind or my ego?" Thus we keep on lifting and lifting the thought, until we rise to a plane where we no longer identify ourselves with the body. The highest form of healing is when we do not think of the body at all. We do not seek the Spirit for a little health or a little prosperity. We love the Spirit wholly for the sake of Spirit; yet every time we come in touch with it, we are re-vivified.

Before we reach this exalted state, however, there are certain scientific systems which will aid us. In Raja-Yoga and Hatha-Yoga, where health comes first, we are told that we must have a proper physical vehicle with which to work out our perfection. One way to do this is through the control of breath. The breath is the medium of life. When a man ceases to breathe, we say he is dead. By the understanding and application of the science of right breathing we can keep this body in a healthy condition; because by our breathing we control the *Prana* or life-force. As long as this life-force continues to circulate evenly and steadily, perfect rhythm or balance will be maintained in our system and we shall enjoy good health. We know, however, from our own experience how dependent our breath is on the mind. The slightest mental agitation will destroy the regularity of the breath and cause disturbance in the system. If we are not able to bring any counteracting influence, this disturbance may develop into definite pain or disease. If, on the contrary, we can control our breathing, we shall restore the equilibrium of our mind and thereby safeguard our health.

When we acquire complete breath-control, we have such a store of *Prana* at our command that we can send it to any part of our organism, where there may be pain or distress, and reinvigorate it. Also we can trasmit it to others. This explains the sudden cures by laying on of hands and all forms of magnetic healing. One must be very careful, however, in permitting this kind of treatment; for unless the channel is pure, it may lead to serious consequences. A man may have a certain magnetic power and yet not be free from selfish personal motives. If we bring ourselves under the domination of such influences we shall impede our higher growth, although for the time being we may gain relief from our physical ailment.

If we do not think rightly and live rightly, we cannot have health; because we generate a poison in our system by our wrong thoughts and actions which must culminate in disease. Even medical science has come to recognize that any strong passion, such as vehement anger or bitter hatred, may lead to serious illness. If on the other hand we live absolutely in accordance with spiritual laws, we need not concern ourselves about our health. We shall be filled spontaneously with life from the central storehouse; for whenever man can rise above the little self and become united with that which is universal and cosmic, there is no limit to his strength. It is because we fail to keep ourselves connected with this storehouse that our vitality is so often depleted. We forget whence comes our supply; and for this reason we must have fixed hours to remind us. The tendency of materialism is to make us forget. It holds out promises of prosperity, but it cuts the very root of the tree of life. If we care merely for one flower or fruit of a tree and water that instead of pouring the water on the root, the whole tree withers. In the same way only as we water the root of the tree of life by daily conscious communion with the Spirit, does it grow and become productive. When we are suffering, we must search within ourselves and see whether we are connected with the Source or not. If the connection is broken, we may know that that is the cause of our ailments. Sometimes we are unable to establish the connection for ourselves and then we are forced to seek help outside; but this cannot be effective until we have within us a certain amount of harmony and purity; for it is not all who can be helped, but only those who are open-hearted.

It is expected of every spiritual teacher that his very word or touch will be full of healing. But whence comes this power? Through divine communion and complete surrender. He merges the little self in the infinite Self; and when any one can rise above all sense of illness or bodily limitation, trusting wholly in the Divine, then whatever flows through him must bring unfailing blessing. A saint says to a man, "Be thou whole," and at once he becomes whole. Why? Because constant contemplation of truth has made the saint truthful; nothing false dwells in his heart; his will has become part of the divine Will; therefore whatever he says must come true, because he has no thought apart from God. The power of the Spirit destroys all the limitations of human life, just as the light of the sun destroys darkness. When we come to the threshold of Truth, our whole being is filled with power. All the Great Ones are full of this power and they have it because they do not ask anything for themselves. They give themselves wholly to the infinite Power, hence they have power in abundance. Whenever a Manifestation of the light and love of God appears, he destroys all sorrow. He becomes a constant solace to mankind, and people gather round him to be healed of the wounds of this world. A saint or Saviour is always marked by his healing grace, but we must never forget that this power is God-given and should never be used for material ends. Whoever would exercise it must always remember that it is of God and that he must keep himself as a pure, clear channel through which the divine Power can flow.

The healer must feel himself wholly an instrument of God. The gift of healing the sick and comforting the afflicted comes from a divine Source, and can only come to one who is absolutely free from self-consciousness and calculation. It must be used silently, without any noise or thought of recognition. As soon as any ulterior personal motive enters, the power diminishes; for these things cannot go hand in hand—the power of God and the ambition of man. Whenever we try to use a lofty Ideal for an ordinary purpose, like money-making or self-aggrandizement, it must become degraded. In India spiritual healing has always been known, but it has never been used as a profession or as a means of livelihood. It has been practised silently and the personal element has always been eliminated. In consequence, although there are thousands of instances of healing in the lives of India's Great Teachers, very few have been recorded. Christ, too, said more than once: "Go and tell no man." Often people quote from the Bible that the laborer is worthy of his hire; but the only true wage for spiritual service can be increased spiritual power and inward joy, not any material gain. The motive in all such work must be selfless love. If our heart burns with the desire to help humanity, we shall not think of anything else. The more we feel the presence of God and the less our thought dwells on worldly gain or loss, the more shall we be filled with the spirit of love and without love there cannot be any true healing.

At every moment we have within us the possibility of health and ill-health; and when some one rouses health in us, he only rekindles the fire of life already there. Though we may obtain help from outside, we can never be permanently helped until we gain knowledge of our own true nature. Therefore Vedanta teaches "Know thy Self," because knowledge of the higher Self is death to all the afflictions of the world. If we can gain conscious possession of the healing power within us, we do not need to look to others for help; we can heal ourselves. There are various methods by which we may accomplish self-healing,—rigid and continual denial of disease, constructive affirmations, and concentration of the mind on a counteracting influence. These may be effective, but all methods of self-exertion are fraught with the subtle danger of egotism. The highest and safest form of self-healing is when we do it involuntarily through meditation; that is, we abandon all thought of sickness or health, we lift our mind beyond all mundane things and strive to enter into the divine Presence. When we are able to do this even for a moment, although we may not ask to be restored, yet we are made whole.

Meditation has wonderful healing power. Sleep gives a hint of it. When we fall asleep, we forget all our suffering, but infinitely more true is this in meditation. In meditation we are conscious only of the infinite One; and when our thought is wrapped up in that One, our whole being is flooded with new life and strength. Only when we are primarily of

God and secondarily of the world do we rise above all our miseries and are healed of all our mortal pains. As the Upanishads declare: "The unbounded Infinite is bliss, there is no bliss in the finite. The Infinite is immortal, the finite is mortal. He who has reached this, if blind, ceases to be blind; if wounded, ceases to be wounded; if afflicted, ceases to be afflicted."

II.

CONTROL OF BREATH AND HEALING

The Sun of Righteousness arises with healing in His wings.—*Malachi.*

I am suddenly renewed. I am changed. I am plunged into ineffable peace. My mind is full of gladness; all my past wretchedness and pain is forgot.—*Hugh of St. Victor.*

Journey towards God even though you be lamed or crippled in soul. To wait for healing is to lose time. —*Sufi.*

THIS God-given life of ours is sacred and full of infinite possibilities; but being unaware of this fact, we live half blindfolded, accepting every condition which confronts us, because we feel powerless to counteract it. Thus we deprive ourselves of the health, happiness and freedom which are our rightful heritage. Among the psychologists of ancient India a great effort was made to discover methods by which all the baser tendencies and impulses inherent in our nature might be overcome. Taking first the physical, they tried to make the body so rhythmic and harmonious that it would not create any obstacle to the free flowing of the life-force within. Breath became the chief factor in doing this. We live so long as we breathe. If a man can breathe in such a way that he can keep his reservoir of vital energy full, then he will have an inexhaustible supply of strength. But very few of us know how to do this. We simply inhale and exhale, without consciousness of what we are doing. It is not an action over which we have any apparent control. The early Indian teachers, however, tried to formulate a science of breath, recognizing that it was the medium of life.

It is through the breath that we convey the life-force, which they called *Prana*. This *Prana* is so subtle that we cannot lay our fingers upon it. When we seek to study it, we see nothing; we are unable even to describe or analyze it. But this we know,—that as long as we are able to inhale that force, so long we live; when breathing stops, we cease to live. Therefore, these teachers sought to make a scientific study of the control of breath. They found that by breath control we can check the waste of bodily energy and acquire sound health. But that was not all. They discovered also that apart from its effect on bodily health, it constituted a potent factor in our spiritual development.

Ordinary breathing exercises help us to cleanse our inner nature. We know that whenever we are ill or when our body is disturbed in any way, we do not breathe normally; the rhythm is lost. Then, because we breathe irregularly, we are exhausted. Whenever we are nervous, ill or feverish, there is great waste in the system; and it is chiefly due to this irregular breathing, which invariably weakens us. If we will learn to regulate the breath, we can counteract these conditions; and if at the same time we also concentrate our thought, we can gain wonderful control over our physical life. Thought has a vital influence on our bodily health and especially on the breath. Whenever we are under any great mental excitement, we see how abnormal and erratic the breath becomes. Whenever, on the other hand, our mind is exalted and peaceful, our breath grows very quiet and rhythmic.

It is not possible for me here to take up any intricate methods of breathing, although the various methods of controlling the breath and thereby restoring the equilibrium of the body were made a great science in Indian psychology. It recognized that this body is the instrument through which we have to work out our salvation. If it is out of order, it becomes a serious hindrance. When the body is disturbed, it is difficult to forget it; and if we are constantly thinking of the body, we have no time to think of higher things.

A healthy person is one who is least conscious of his body. Therefore the object of all breath-control is to make ourselves as little conscious of our physical condition as possible. This cannot be done by directing our mental force on every little ache or pain, but by putting the body in tune with higher ideals of life and creating a proper rhythm.

Those early investigators, however, did not pay undue attention to the physical constitution, because after all, the body is only an instrument. Yet they were very strict in all their bodily habits, and because of this they attained great heights in their psychological and spiritual research. If people practise breathing exercises merely with the idea of gaining health or some material advantage, they will achieve very little. Those who take up these practices are expected to live pure, chaste lives; to be very strict in their eating, drinking, recreation and association; and to be free from selfish, unworthy motives. In every way they are supposed to cultivate tranquillity and self-control. How few are willing to do this! Yet without observing these simple rules, we cannot expect any benefit from the practice of Yoga.

Here in the Occident some, carried away by the wonderful results which Yoga promises and yet unwilling to conform with the fundamental principles of right-thinking, purity and self-control, have met with disastrous results. This has led to the erroneous belief that Yoga is dangerous and unsuited to the Occidental temperament. The danger lies wholly in the misuse of the study. The practice of Yoga quickens our latent finer forces, and unless we have the right motive and the knowledge to direct them through the right channels, they necessarily create havoc in our organism; just as a strong medicine, which has curative powers, will injure if not properly administered.

Certain breathing exercises are practised daily by many in India to cleanse their inner organism, just as they take a bath to cleanse the outer body. There are also other exercises to freshen and prepare for meditation, by bringing the whole system into rhythm. Such practices are not only cleansing to the body, but quieting to the mind. Breath is life. When we inhale, if we hold the thought that we are filling ourselves with *Prana* or vital energy; and when we exhale, that we are throwing off all the waste from the system, we cannot fail to be cleansed even by our ordinary breathing. We all know that we live by breathing, by filling our physical organism with oxygen; if added to this we have a certain spiritual understanding regarding these things, we can do much to help ourselves.

When we are tired and feel the need of relaxation or when we are nervous and restless, if we will fix our mind on some lofty thought and begin to breathe rhythmically—that is, breathe in and out on an even count—we shall restore our equilibrium and grow peaceful. This is a scientific fact. It may not seem to have any direct spiritual bearing, but it undoubtedly helps us to gain spiritual ends. That is why the ancient Indo-Aryans laid so much emphasis on these practices. They knew that unless a man could control his body and bring it to a state of equilibrium, he could not focus his mind on the higher facts of life.

Also they discovered that if a man could fill his own system full of *Prana,* he could then impart it to others and thus heal and help. Highly developed spiritual beings often do this quite unconsciously by a touch or a glance or a word. But they are able to do it only because of their selflessness. It is this which differentiates ordinary healing from spiritual healing, as we find it in the lives of the great saints and Saviours. In the ordinary practice of healing there is a distinct consciousness of individual effort; while in the higher method there is a total absence of self-consciousness. The true healer must feel that the power flows through him. He must have no thought of self. He must not care for name or fame or material gain. True spiritual healing is only possible when all such ideas are absent.

In India they recognize the power of healing and have studied it as a science, but it is not so much discussed as in the West. The monistic system of healing there, is much like the Christian Science conception here. It does not recognize any bodily condition as real. No affliction, it declares, can touch the soul. It holds one idea only: that the Infinite is One without a second, and "Thou art That," free from all impurity, free from all disease, death and misery. Of course if we can rise to such heights of consciousness, everything will roll away from us; but it means a very lofty flight. If there is no body, naturally we cannot treat a body; so the true monist cannot deal with either good health or ill health.

The idea of healing which we find in the lives of Jesus the Christ, Sri Krishna, Buddha, Lord Gouranga and other great Saviours is the same. There is only one ideal—that the Divine can work wonders through us. Are we willing to give ourselves to that divine Being? Are we really willing to offer our hands, our heart, our mind, everything we possess, our every faculty and gift, wholly without any thought of return? If we are, then even miracles of healing may be accomplished through us. There are here and there people who succeed in eliminating all their egoistic sense. They offer themselves wholly to God, and God works through them. They do not ask anything in return. And this is the only safe form of healing. The other methods are merely experiments—sometimes they work and sometimes they do not. Or sometimes they seem to work, but the cure is not permanent.

An example of true healing is to be seen in St. Francis' life, when He cured the perverse leper not only of his leprosy, but also of his evil temper. Seeing that the other brothers could not content him by their service, St. Francis Himself went to him. "God give thee peace, my brother most dear," He said to him tenderly. The leper replied: "What peace may I have of God, who hath made me rotten altogether?" "My little son, have patience,"

St. Francis gave answer, "for the infirmities of the body are given by God in this world for the salvation of souls, seeing that they bring great blessing when they are borne patiently." Then He prayed fervently for the sick man and bathed him in warm water scented with sweet smelling herbs. As His loving hands passed over the afflicted body, all the sores were healed. Mind and heart also were made whole, so that the man began to rejoice and glorify God. Unless the cure reaches to the soul, to-day the pain may be gone and to-morrow something may happen to bring it back again; just as to-day we may relieve a poor man by giving him a piece of bread, but to-morrow he is hungry once more.

The relief we receive on the physical plane cannot be permanent. Only when we gain direct knowledge of Spirit do we find a true remedy. The great spiritual teachers may have wrought miracles in healing men's bodies, but they did more than this. They produced a lasting impression on their lives, and they did this by the power of Spirit. That alone can heal the wounds of the heart. It also heals the mind of all doubt, of all sorrow and darkness. The majority of mankind is more or less in an unhealthy condition, either of body or mind. The greatest disease of the mind is doubt. Even when our body is strong, are we free from doubt—doubt of God, doubt of the soul, doubt of the permanent realities of life? If not, then we cannot enjoy true health, and the only thing which can cure us is a revelation of Truth.

We all have great opportunities, but we do not know always how to make use of these opportunities. We have wonderful blessings, but we do not know how to retain them. This comes from our lack of preparation. Therefore we must prepare ourselves spiritually. Let us prepare our body; let us prepare our mind; and let us be ready to accept humbly all the help which comes to us, no matter through what channel. Only as we accept help from every source with openness of heart and an ardent spirit, can we restore ourselves to a normal condition; and a normal condition of life is reached when our body, our mind, our whole being responds naturally to the call of Spirit and is able to radiate the power of the Infinite. You ask, "Is it possible for us to do this?" Yes. But we must reverse the order of our life; and instead of being so full of craving for material things, we must be filled with yearning for spiritual things. When our heart is filled with such yearning, then alone shall we feel the reality of the blessed Spirit and realize the fullness of life.

III.

THE SOURCE OF HEALING POWER

Where self is, truth cannot be. Self is death and truth is life. The cleaving to self is a perpetual dying, while moving in the truth is partaking of Nirvana which is life everlasting.—*Buddha.*

If any man will come after me, let him deny himself, and take up his cross daily and follow me. For whosoever will save his life, shall lose it; but whosoever will lose his life for my sake, the same shall save it.—*Jesus the Christ.*

LIFE makes one living; absence of life means death. Light reveals; absence of light enshrouds in darkness. If through prayer or faith or devotion or meditation a person succeeds in uniting himself with the Source of life and light and being united, becomes a medium through which these may flow, he is able to restore and illumine others. This is the way the Great Ones have always healed. They themselves possess life in such abundance that they have the power to impart it for the time being to another;

but the cure cannot be permanent unless the person's spiritual nature is awakened.

Help is lasting only when it shows us how to bring ourselves into union with the Source; and when we have learned to do that, we have no further need of healing, because there is a constant flux of life in us which keeps us well. What impedes that flow now? It is our attitude of mind —doubt, despair, all the various phases of worldly consciousness, which make us feel more united with the body than with Spirit. The more we think of the body, the less are we conscious of that which sustains the body.

Vedic teaching declares with dynamic force: The soul of man is eternal, unbounded; it is not bound by body or senses or pain or afflictions. It is free, pure and perfect. If through contemplation we are able to lift our thought to the plane where this is a reality, we are restored. If we can separate ourselves—not through death, but through higher reflection—from our body-consciousness, at once we are released from bodily pain. We must not do it, however, as beggars, asking for health or physical comfort. It must be done with superior feeling and understanding. We must seek the higher for the sake of the higher, not merely in order tc benefit the lower nature; otherwise we shall miss our end.

One who is always seeking material benefits rarely has his desires satisfied; but to one who does not seek them, they come easily and abundantly. How strange seems the law! When we study it, however, we find that it is neither strange nor unjust. The cosmic universe gives to each one according to his fitness, and a man makes himself fit to receive by his attitude of mind and by his feeling. If he is consumed with material desires, he blocks the way; no higher blessings can reach him. He has not made himself fit. The cosmic law never makes a mistake. It never gives anything to the unfit.

All real healing is quite involuntary. It comes from the central reservoir of life, and that reservoir is shut off when our consciousness is fixed on the physical. If we are overcome by aches and pains and look to material means only for relief, this may come or it may not; but even if it comes, it will be merely temporary. There can be permanent healing only when we turn to the Source of all supply, which is within. We must learn to retire within ourselves when there is any trouble. Whatever overtakes us—whether it be physical illness, nervous excitement or mental disturbance—we must not reach out to the external world for help; we must try rather to make ourselves more fit for the manifestation of the divine

Spirit. If we can draw close to the cosmic Source within ourselves, we shall be relieved from our aches and pains and darkness.

That inner Light, the wise men say, is the cure for all ailments; but we do not seek help there. We seek everywhere else. We turn to the spiritual Source as a last resort. Yet until we bring ourselves into contact with That, we shall have no real peace or rest or strength. Meditation therefore becomes a vital factor in all healing. I have known many instances of involuntary cures through meditation, and it is easy to explain them. The power of meditation enables one to transcend the physical, to forget the limited self with its endless concerns and occupations, which now absorb and distract the mind.

What part of us is suffering? Can the real man be touched by any of these afflictions? Sages and seers tell us that the real is undying and undecaying. "Sword cannot pierce it, fire cannot burn it, water cannot wet it, air cannot dry it." It is immutable, imperishable. This brings before our mind another picture. If we can feel its reality, immediately we are restored. But mere words cannot do it. The method of positive mental affirmation may bring a moment's relief and upliftment, but any lasting result must be based on feeling. We must feel the presence of that indestructible essence; and if we actually do feel it, we cannot be saturated at the same time with bodily consciousness. If our sufferings are due to matter, then the remedy must be sought in the spiritual; and the more we learn to turn towards that, the more our life is balanced. Instead of giving way to a feeling of helplessness when afflictions come upon us, we should take a firm stand in spiritual thought.

We must not imagine that all bodily disease is the result of wrong-doing. There are those who think that whenever there is any physical disturbance, it must be due to sin and they are ashamed to have it known. On the contrary the disturbance may be the outer sign of an active cleansing process, which is preparing us for a new spiritual awakening. It is a very great thing to have a healthy body, but a healthy body alone does not lead one to the loftiest pinnacle of spiritual attainment. There are plenty of healthy animals and there are also plenty of healthy people who have not begun to approach the state of spiritual consciousness. Physical health is not the end and aim of life. Bodily healing is not always a blessing. It may even prove a drawback. Suffering also has a purpose in our experience. It loosens the hold of the flesh on us and enables our mind to rise to a higher plane of consciousness. Sometimes an illness brings a lesson of which we have need. People are awakened often to higher thought and ideals through bodily afflictions or through misfortune. A person who is full of aspiration learns both through good fortune and ill fortune; he learns equally through physical disease and through health. There are many different disciplines in life; and if we do not have an all-round experience, our consciousness remains incomplete.

This does not mean that we should deliberately invite ill health. Health is a great blessing. A healthy body is an undeniable advantage in our spiritual pursuits; but we must not let ourselves become absorbed in the idea of health as an end in itself. The best form of health is where we are least conscious that we have a body. When we are really healthy, we do not think about the body at all, our feet scarcely touch the ground; but when we are thinking constantly of the body, that is not a healthy attitude of mind or a healthy state of body. We should try to regulate our life in such a way that we do not violate the law, because nothing contributes more towards good health than an orderly life of moderation. We must be careful not to be carried away by minor details. We must desire a strong body wholly that we may express Divinity within us, and that we may love and serve the Ideal. If we do not use our health to this end, we are bound again and again by physical fetters.

Meditation is invaluable even for our bodily welfare, because it gives us balance. It quiets our nerves and brings our muscles to a state of tranquillity. Often this is done involuntarily. We must not begin to meditate on Truth, however, with the idea that we may get health or happiness or prosperity. Not at all. We must meditate on Truth for the love of Truth; and when that is fully awakened in us, it will so consume our heart and thought that we shall rise above all material considerations and in an instant we shall be restored.

This is the real method by which we gain health. It is not done merely by turning our thought on our head when we have a headache, or on our heart if we have a heartache. This is a very primary way of trying to relieve pain. We drive it out from one part and it goes to another. To-day we free our mind from one grief and to-morrow again something may happen to disturb it. We do not get rid of our troubles and ills in life in that way. It is done by lifting our thought, by fastening our heart to that which is Unbounded and Eternal. The Vedic Rishis have taught us this higher method. They declare to man that there is no permanent happiness in the finite, the changing, the fleeting. That which is infinite and everlasting, That alone is the Source of real happiness and blessing. We must bind our hearts to That. In That is the only permanent cure for all disease, because It carries us beyond ignorance, beyond selfishness, beyond the unreal.

Intellectually we may conceive that our soul is perfect, pure, free from sickness and death, but we cannot hold to the idea when something goes wrong. We are troubled and unhappy in spite of our theoretical conception. We are unable to maintain our peace and our equilibrium. It is not a matter of a philosophic theory, but of knowing directly, of feeling, of being in tune with Spirit. An intellectual conception, no matter how big or how comforting it may appear to be, will never support us really unless we have made it our own through contemplation.

This contemplation, however, is not an abstraction. It does not make us visionary or turn our thoughts to emptiness. No. It makes the Unseen real and tangible to us. So long as we depend on a physical source only, we are deprived of many rich blessings. But when we go inward, we touch the real source of wholeness. We may think out hundreds of external ways to safeguard ourselves, but still we find we are not safe. The real safety of man is within himself. When we find that inner Refuge, we shall know how to rise above all afflictions and calamities and we shall be able to help others rise above them.

We must not give up. We all have latent within us a love for the true, for the perfect. We all want that which is unlimited and eternal. There is an inner longing which drives us constantly. Even the mistakes we make are due to our effort to find true happiness; but we seek it in the finite, so we suffer. The Eternal is not to be found in the perishable. If we desire a real cure for our ills, physical or mental, we must seek it in the Imperishable. The Source of life is not outside and separate from us. It is within us. The kingdom of God is within and we are told to seek that first, then all else will follow. Do we believe it? If we do, then we shall turn towards it naturally. Whenever we feel any lack or any distress, instead of turning towards the external, we shall turn towards the internal.

A wise man goes within himself in his joys and his sorrows. He strives to unite himself more closely with his Source in every experience of life. He knows that all his power comes from there and he takes no credit to himself. No man can become a channel of divine power so long as his ego is in the ascendancy. He may be able to heal temporarily, but it will not last. To become a true channel he must attune himself with God through humility, through purity, through an utter lack of self-consciousness.

Whenever we feel turbulence in our mind or disturbance in our body, if we can fix our thought on our spiritual Source and give Nature a chance to restore us by trying to forget the cause of our pain, we shall be healed without any outside help. God is our common property. We do not have to gain access to Him through any book or minister or church or healer. All that we need is purity of thought, an open heart and sincere childlike longing. When we have these, all darkness vanishes quickly and healing takes place. When we touch the reservoir of life, the storehouse of *Prana* or vital energy, all our weakness must disappear. Some accomplish this by a definite system of thought;

others do it through simple faith and devotion.

There are many simple people who by mere faith and ardent devotion have performed what we call miracles; but they are not miracles in the sense that they could not happen to any one. Healing comes wholly through fitness. Let us all strive to make ourselves fit for the manifestation of divine power. Let us make it our first duty always to turn towards that inner Source for all our needs. Let us tune ourselves in such a way that we shall never be a jarring note in the cosmic harmony. If we learn to keep ourselves in tune, there will be no need of healing; because when our body and mind and soul are attuned to the central spiritual power, this physical machine will run smoothly and we shall be scarcely conscious that we have a body. Our whole thought will be turned towards God.

IV.

HEALING OF BODY AND MIND

Convinced that he is not the body and that he does not possess it, the wise man attains oneness with his higher Self, and casts aside all thought of himself as the doer.—*Samhita.*

It is more necessary for the soul to be cured than the body, for it is better to die than to live unworthily. —*Epictetus.*

The soul gives sight to the eyes. He who gives sight to the soul is the great Lord. Therefore one should worship Him with supreme love who does kindness to the soul.—*Saiva Siddhantam.*

Live in this world as if God and your soul only were in it; that your heart may be a captive to no earthly thing.—*St. John of the Cross.*

MAN'S life is inter-related. His physical life is so absolutely dependent on his moral and his spiritual life that unless he pay proper heed to these, he can never hope to be healthy. Whenever we violate the spiritual law and try to find a short cut to happiness, the fibre of our moral being is injured and we begin to feel pains and aches in the physical body. When these conditions continue and we do not try to remove them, a mark is made on the mind. Doubt, despair, despondency arise and these react again on the body. The only healing which can be effective then, will be one which brings a regenerating influence into the mind and restores it to its normal state.

How does spiritual healing take place? A sceptic says that it does not take place at all, it is a myth; but it could not be conceived by human minds unless it were founded to some extent at least on fact. All history is filled with accounts of such healing. We read of it in the life of Krishna, in the life of Buddha, in the life of Christ, of Lord Gouranga, of St. Francis. It is love conquering brute force. The force which is moving in the direction of evil is reversed suddenly and becomes a power for good. This is what I call reversion. A man can never be converted by violence or by mere persuasion. He can be transformed permanently only by a spiritual influx which is so redeeming, so life-giving, so healing, that when he comes in contact with it, he is re-made. Whenever this influence falls upon a receptive heart, it cleanses and exalts the whole nature as a natural sequence; disturbing physical conditions fall away and mental distresses vanish. This is the only real process of healing.

In India spiritual healing has never been practised as a profession, because there they know that God's power cannot be used for any material advantage or with any sense of egotism. Only when we have no ulterior motive, no thought of self, do we become direct channels for it. Our heart must be full of purity, of selfless devotion, of real love for humanity. If on the contrary we take up healing as a profession, expecting a definite return from it, the supply is cut off. Every individual has the right and the power to connect himself with the infinite Source and be filled constantly with fresh life and understanding. In accomplishing this the mind plays a greater part than the body. We are all anxious to maintain physical health. There is not a person who is not interested in possessing it. But in order to have it, we must acquire a well-ordered mind; because our thoughts and feelings and aspirations will produce either good health or ill health in our body. You may ask why do so many good people suffer? Suffering is not a curse; bodily illness is not necessarily a punishment. Sometimes it comes to purify and strengthen us Therefore those who have deeper understanding strive to make the best use of illness. Bodily suffering becomes a blessing when it teaches us to transcend outer conditions and to turn to the soul within.

Each of us is a living part of the Whole, a direct descendant of Godhead; and when we become truly aware of this, it cures all our ailments. In my own life I have known of extreme cases, pronounced hopeless by physicians, which were healed by a mere touch. Yet there was no miracle about it. It was the transmission of a spiritual power which accomplished it. If any man can resign himself absolutely and unreservedly to the Will of God, in a moment he will be made whole, and he will be able to heal others. The healing takes place by the natural process of life. Ordinarily we seek relief through roundabout ways; we seek all our consolation and help from outside; but if we can turn directly within to our own inward resources, we shall get results which will amaze us. The reservoir of life is inexhaustible. So long as we go on crying: "My strength has failed, my usefulness is gone, my faculties have lost their power to act!" we shut ourselves away from the

Fountainhead. The fact that we are in that state shows that we have detached ourselves from the Source of life. A branch withers quickly when it is severed from the root, and the root of every human life is God.

If we do not believe that God is the Source of our life, in what can we believe? Can we believe in changeable mundane things and hope for perfect health or happiness through them? No. We may try to reverse the order of our life, but the Cosmic Law does not reverse its order. That is why the fundamental principle of attainment must be always: "Seek ye first the kingdom of Truth, all other things shall be added unto you." Why is it we find this so difficult to follow? Because we do not really believe in it. We may pretend loyalty to a religion, we may pretend to have lofty aspirations, we may pretend devotion to all sorts of ideals with high-sounding names, but mere pretending will not lead us anywhere. We must have real love for an Ideal in our hearts; then not only do we elevate ourselves, but we are able to bring constant benefit to the world. We see this in the lives of the Great Ones. A Buddha, a St. Francis, a man who possesses nothing, becomes a great power. He revolutionizes human society. Even material weapons drop powerless before him. In the life of Gautama Buddha we read that once the priests out of jealousy plotted to do away with Him and engaged some wicked men to take His life. The men came to Him with drawn swords, but they were disarmed by His gentle exalted bearing and refused to do Him harm. If our faith in the all-conquering power of love is equally genuine, we also shall be victorious over evil. But there can be no compromise. In all circumstances, whether pleasing or unpleasing, we must hold fast to our ideal of love. That love never fails to cure both mind and body. It was by this love that St. Francis conquered and transformed the hearts of the three robbers.

Once three robbers came to the monastery asking for food. Brother Angelo, knowing who they were, drove them away with harsh words. St. Francis, returning from His daily round of begging, heard of it and, sad at heart, He reproached the brother for his lack of loving-kindness. "Take thou this wallet of bread," He said, "and this flask of wine which I have begged, and seek out the robbers. Kneel before them humbly and ask their pardon for thy harshness. Beseech them in my name to offend God no longer by evil-doing. Tell them, if they will do this, that I promise to provide for their needs. Give them to eat, then return hither." Brother Angelo found the robbers, and while they were eating of St. Francis' alms, their hearts were so softened they began to be overwhelmed with remorse for their evil deeds. "Let us go to St. Francis," they said to one another, "and implore Him to save us from our many grievous sins." St. Francis received them lovingly, consoled them with many tender hopeful counsels, and they all became devout members of the Order.

We often say: "I would like to be unselfish; I would like to think noble thoughts, but it is an impossibility for me." Why should it be an impossibility? If the mind is capable of thinking ignoble thought, it has an equal capacity for loving, constructive thought. It is a question of training. Unless we train our body and mind and readjust our habits, it is useless to uphold visionary ideals, which remain mere theories for us. We should be grateful that difficulties come sometimes, because they test our sincerity. They show us whether we are standing on the solid foundation of spiritual conviction. If we are not, it is better that we find it out. Ailments come, misfortunes come; but they prove to be curses only when we fall under their sway. When we are not crushed by them, we rise up with greater strength. This conquest is the greatest thing man can hope for and it comes through the power of the Spirit. Wealth cannot buy it, or learning. Sometimes rather these hinder our efforts, because they confuse our mind and destroy the purity of our vision. If we would have either health or wisdom, we must keep to simplicity and directness in our mental and bodily habits.

The story is told that when Lord Buddha was preaching in the neighborhood of Shravasti, a man of great wealth came to Him and said: "World-honored

Master, forgive me that I do not prostrate before you with proper reverence; but I suffer miserably from obesity, drowsiness, excessive lethargy and other complaints, which make it impossible for me to move without pain." Buddha, observing the luxuries with which the man was surrounded, asked him: "Have you a desire to know the real cause of your unhappy state?" The man assented and Buddha continued: "There are five things which produce the conditions from which you suffer:—opulent dinners, love of sleep, love of pleasure, thoughtlessness and lack of occupation. Begin to exercise control at your meals, and take upon yourself some occupation which will employ your abilities and make you useful to your fellow-men. In doing this you will prolong your life."

The rich man heard the words of the Blessed One and, having regained his lightness of body and buoyancy of mind, he returned to the world-honored One afoot and without attendants. "Master," he said, "you have cured my bodily ailments. I come now to seek the enlightenment of my mind." And the Blessed One said: "The worldling nourishes his body, but the wise man nourishes his soul. He who indulges in the satisfaction of his appetites works his own destruction; but he who walks in the path of self-discipline will not only gain salvation from sin, but prolong his life." This may not seem a great miracle. Buddha made only the simplest suggestions. He did not lay His hand on the man and cure him at once, although He might have done that. But such instances of sudden healing are to me not more miraculous than this one, because this has the element of rebuilding the moral fibre; and until that is accomplished, no matter how much we may try to help any one, it will not prove a lasting blessing.

One can be cured by the laying on of hands, by prayer, by transmission of spiritual force, provided the healer is pure, exalted and free from every selfish motive. Often those who are the most powerful healers are not conscious that they are healing. Nor do they wish their power to be known or recognized. Why? Because they are not willing to mix their spirit of consecration to God with the cheaper materials of self-glorification, egotism and vanity. If you are interested in healing, do it; but keep yourself out of it. Bring in God's power and all things will be made whole for you. Do not resort to trivial methods; that is, when you have a little bodily ache or pain, do not focus your thought on it in the hope of escaping from it; or when you think you need a new dress or a new hat, do not expend your precious mental energies in trying to obtain them.

Concentrating your mind to satisfy trifling desires proves always a great detriment to your higher unfoldment, and you should do your utmost by the practice of discrimination to avoid this mis-step. There are people who by concentrating realize their material ambitions, and they imagine that they possess superior spiritual power, but this is merely a snare, which cheats them of true attainment.

How do you know that what you obtain is good for you? Oftentimes we find that it is not beneficial for us to have a great deal of material prosperity. We may like the soft conditions of life; but they are not always wholesome for our higher nature. What we need is a mind which can stand firm in all circumstances; a mind which is brave and heroic. True heroism is born of Spirit, never of material conditions.

Real strength does not come from the flesh, it comes only when flesh is connected with Spirit; then we can go through the greatest ordeal unmoved. All that we crave we shall receive in unbounded supply, when we know how to use it for our own good and for the good of our fellowmen. We would all like to possess happiness and power, but these do not come to us because we are not big enough to take them. We must cultivate bigness and inwardness.

We cannot realize the highest happiness so long as we are thinking of ourselves only, of our own needs and gratifications. Not until the sun of wisdom shines and melts away these selfish limitations, not until then will rise from within our true power, which is inexhaustible. An unrivalled passage in the Upanishads tells us that in the vastness of infinitude alone lies the fullness of happiness for man; never in the finite. Men go on groping here and there to gratify their desires; and they often gain what they covet, but it never satisfies their deep craving. We enter into our true state of being only when we forget ourselves; when we cease to believe that our body is given us for our gratification, that our mind and acquirements are for ourselves.

We must lose all self-consciousness in the great thought that we are instruments of God; we must feel that our body must be kept clean and holy as a shrine for the dwelling-place of Divinity. If we keep uppermost in our mind these higher concepts of life, we shall refrain from doing what is ignoble. Do we wish to be strong, do we wish to be happy? If we do, then we must plant the seeds of constructive thought in our hearts. We must remember constantly that no matter what happens on the physical plane, there is a dominant ruler within, the Spirit, and that Spirit can never be vanquished. When we are able to take this stand, we can overcome every obstacle.

Why do people become selfish? Why are they guilty of unworthy acts which harm others? It is because they have lost this lofty point of view. Their whole life is centred in their flesh, in sensation, in immediate bodily concerns. But let them extend their vision, let them project their thought beyond mere physical boundary lines, and a new inner consciousness will dawn in them. Their body may still have its limitations, their material surroundings may continue to be disturbing; in spite of all this, they will not be moved from the state of tranquillity they have found. This is only possible when we bring spiritual consciousness into our life. When we feel that we are direct descendants of the Infinite, when this conviction is firmly established in our hearts, then are we made whole. It is the life which brings healing. It is entering into the inner realm of consciousness where we are restored naturally. When our thought is filled with Spirit, all must be well with us; because where Spirit shines unobstructed, there is life; there can be no sickness or suffering.

V.

HEALING IN MEDITATION

That happiness which belongs to a mind, which by deep meditation has been washed clean from all impurity and has entered within the Self, cannot be described by words; it can be felt by the inward power only.—*Maitrayana-Brahmana-Upanishad.*

Now what most contributes to the growth of these wings of the soul is meditation, by which we learn little by little to wean our affections from earthly things, and to get a habit of contemplating the things that are immaterial and intelligible, and to shake off the pollutions it has contracted by its union with the terrestrial and mortal body. And, indeed, by these advantages it revives in some manner, it rouses up itself, it is filled with divine vigor and reunites itself to the Intelligent Perfection within.—*Hierocles.*

WHENEVER we are in trouble physically, or distressed mentally, we seek for help in the outside world, but very seldom we think that there is already within us the most potent and infallible remedy. Meditation opens to us such a source of remedy. It has a decided healing power over both body and mind, but unfortunately the majority of people regard it as a negative state, entirely aloof from our every-day, active life. But it is not so. It is the greatest creative force within us. Consciously and unconsciously we all make use of it. There are certain thoughts which have a hold upon us; we cannot get away from their influence; but whether our meditation is voluntary or involuntary, our mind always takes the imprint of our thoughts. Whenever we are able to keep our mind connected for any length of time with something beautiful and restful, we feel refreshed. A tired person coming in contact with nature becomes rested just by looking at the trees, the flowers and the birds. It is not that he has actually taken anything away from Nature. Nature still stands intact, but the thought has lifted him from his tired bodily conditions and restored him.

People are always striving to avoid physical and nervous reactions, but it is very difficult to get away from them.

Whenever we act, no matter what the action is, it brings reaction and not always a pleasing one. Unless we know how to control this constant action and reaction which is taking place, we must feel the wear and tear of life. How often we hear it said, "I am a complete wreck; I have worked so hard, I have no energy left." It is not by refraining from action that we restore our energy and maintain our health. True healthfulness is something to be found from within. If the mind is diseased, sooner or later the body will feel it, but Nature is inevitably healing in its effect and will reconstruct if left unhindered. Whenever we have a cut or a burn, if we rub it, it becomes worse. A physician will tell you to leave it alone, not to touch it; he will even bandage it up so you will not irritate it. If your eyes are inflamed, your natural tendency is to rub them; but the more you do so, the more inflamed they become. Nature works the same way in our mental ailments. The more we dwell on these things, the more acute they grow; but when we are able to forget them, we are restored.

Whenever we are tired or disturbed, instead of allowing our mind to be full of agitation, if we withdraw it entirely from the source of disturbance, we shall not only have a sense of refreshment, but by disconnecting ourselves in this way from our trouble we shall gain a more correct view of it and be able to find the remedy for it. This is a general principle and not merely to be applied to physical ailments. These ailments are after all not so important as we think. Let us take this question up very frankly. Here in the Occident, especially since the rise of certain modern movements, healing has played a tremendous part. There are some people who hold that unless a person has good health he does not amount to anything; that illness is a great curse. In India there is quite another attitude. There, when a person has a little fever or headache or some other physical ailment, it is not held that he has fallen from grace or that a curse has fallen upon him. On the contrary, it is felt that to be able to meet these conditions with absolute equilibrium, without being afflicted, is a great achievement. If we are able to keep our balance in all circumstances, no matter what comes, affliction will not appear to be affliction, because we shall have a consciousness and a power by which we can cope with everything. Is not that much better than merely trying to follow the path of affirmation? To deny pain when you feel it is a very good practice; but to keep on denying it, if it continues, is to be slightly lacking in a sense of true value.

Body and soul each has its own place in our life, and if we can keep these two separate in our mind, often we can make our adjustment. Whenever something happens on the physical plane, we should not take it as an inevitable finality. Spirit can always transcend bodily limitations. That is one of the great thoughts of the Indo-Aryan school of philosophy. This does not mean that there are no healing methods in India. Healing is one of the most essential elements in her spiritual evolution. It is an accepted thing that one who has risen to a great spiritual height can dispel ignorance, the cause of all illness, by his touch, his word, his very presence. Whenever there is light, there can be no darkness. Healing is accomplished in that way, but another element is introduced in order that people may help themselves instead of depending on others, and that is the element of meditation.

When we are in physical or mental trouble, it is well to forget it sometimes. In the world, when we have any perplexing problems we say: "I want to think it over; I want to sleep on it." In other words, we wish to reflect, to find a clear light before we give our decision. That is exactly what meditation means. The body requires a certain amount of inward recreation which the mind can give. Body and mind, when united, find balance, a sense of rest within. Retired from all worldly disturbance they both grow stronger. Whether we are in public life or following some line of spiritual study, we cannot do without these times of retirement. The nervous disorders of modern life are due not so much to our intensity of action as to our lack of understanding and wrong direction of our energy. We must have balance, and meditation gives us that balance. Without it we cannot maintain our health, our happiness or our peace of mind. One person in a household who maintains his balance becomes a great power. He helps even unconsciously. In this day it is hard for us to believe that any one can instruct without speaking. We believe more in noise than in silence; that is our misfortune. We miss the subtler, the finer, the more beautiful part of life when we merely follow the noisy trend of the world.

In India it has been proved by practice that those who live in rhythm, who have a sense of inner values, are naturally possessed of a meditative mind. They go through life without showing any strain. Sometimes they live many years without wrinkles or any sign of old age. For what causes wrinkles? Wrong meditation; that is, a continual dwelling on anxieties and worries. We may feel that we have very good reason to be anxious, to worry; but have we ever gained anything through it except marred physical health, disturbed mental peace and an atmosphere of unrest, which others feel? Meditation is the means by which we can control both body and mind and keep them turned in the right direction, so that even when we have reason for disturbance, we can quickly adjust and detach ourselves. This is most refreshing. When we are very tired and feel that we have almost come to the breaking point, it is an excellent practice to take a deep breath and close our eyes for a few minutes. But it does not do any good to go through these outer forms if our mind is wandering somewhere. If, however, the mind at the same time can be fixed on a beautiful thought, then both body and mind will feel revived.

It never does us any good to dwell on our ills and ailments, either physical or mental. But great help comes by being able to rise above them. Do not think that we can always do this through mental calculation. We may understand our philosophy perfectly in theory, but the practical application is quite a different thing. If, however, we can apply it practically, we not only rid ourselves of our troubles, we create an atmosphere of peace even in the midst of unrest. There lies the value of noble lives, of people who do not merely theorize, but who live their ideals and radiate them. We can all do the same, but we must do it very quietly. We are more successful when we are quiet about it. On this one point there is a great difference between the Oriental and the Occidental point of view. When an Easterner conceives an idea he goes into retirement. "How selfish!" you may say; "he should come forth and preach it to the world." But he wants first to gain direct and absolute knowledge of it. He is not content to take a truth because he has heard it from some one else. He wishes to verify it and make it his own, so first he meditates upon it and then he acts.

Most people act first and think afterwards. It is a dangerous thing to do. We cannot reverse the order in this way in our daily life and expect something heavenly. That is not possible. Keep your inner and your outer life in unison. When these two are flowing in one current without any cross currents, then indeed we have reached a great height. We should strive to do this so that we may maintain rhythm and harmony within ourselves, and never contradict ourselves. How often you remark: "I did not intend to say that." But if you did not intend to say it and yet your mouth uttered it, that is a terrible defeat. It means you have not the meditative habit by which you can completely adjust your life.

Every particle of our body can be brought so absolutely into rhythm that nothing can go out of harmony. You may say that is not possible in this world of chaos. It seems hopeless; we have many obstacles, but that makes it all the more necessary for us to have this inward practice. We do it in our mind, on the street car, walking along a crowded thoroughfare, on the railroad train, wherever we may be. No one should be able to disturb our thoughts, no one should have any control over our minds, but in order that our mind may be absolutely master of the situation, we need to form the habit of meditation,—meditation on the beautiful, meditation on the true. We should ally ourselves as often as we can and as constantly with the Unbounded and the Infinite. In the Upanishads we are taught that in that which is infinite and unbounded lies happiness, real strength and the fulfillment of life. When we are able to look up to That, not only sometimes but always, we live happily. Can we have any real fullness of life if we are separated from the very root of our existence? Have you ever seen a flower or a branch of a tree survive when it is severed from the root? It is not possible. Meditation teaches us how we may keep ourselves united with the Source of our life. This is our heritage. No one should ever regard himself as so sinful, so degraded and so benighted as not to have access to this Source. It is through our mental distortion that we think we have drifted from the Source, that we are weak, impure and selfish, that we have nothing. We have everything. We are the descendants of the infinite, all-beautiful, all-living Spirit. The more we can form the habit of thinking of this, the greater will grow our inward power. Then we can easily cope with all the little things of life. At no moment shall we feel at a loss. At no moment shall we feel that we have to rob any one or cheat another to gain our happiness, because we ourselves shall have so much that it will not only suffice for our own life, but we will be able to share it with others gladly and abundantly.